CONTENTS

3 Joseph Reed
7 19th Century Architecture
11 St Paul's
15 Lombard Building
19 Bank of Australasia
27 Melbourne Town Hall
35 Baptist Church
37 Scots Church
43 Independent Church
47 Wesley Church
51 Royal Society Building
55 Exhibition Buildings
59 Trades Hall
65 State Library

Melbourne University
71 Ormond College
73 Bank of NSW
77 Gatekeeper's Cottage
83 Timeline
84 Glossary

JOSEPH REED

The architect Joseph Reed was responsible for some of the most notable 19th century public and administrative buildings in the city of Melbourne, many of which can still be seen today. Widely regarded as one of the most influential Victorian-era architects in Australia, his buildings represent the enormous increase in both size and wealth that the city experienced throughout the late 1800s.

The Footpath Guide to Joseph Reed showcases 15 prime examples of Reed's work via an easy walking route throughout Melbourne's CBD and shopping precincts.

Joseph Reed was born in the Parish of Constantine, Cornwall, in 1822.

Educated at nearby Helston grammar school, he soon displayed considerable talent as a draftsman when, at age seventeen, he produced a finely detailed map of the Parish of Sithney for the tithe commissioners.

Reed moved to London to commence his professional architectural training with Thomas Bellamy, followed by an appointment as clerk and architect to George Henry Boscawen, 2nd Earl and 5th Viscount of Falmouth. Work included additions to the Earl's mansion, Tregothnan House, and the design and construction of various other buildings on the estate and surrounding properties. The unmarried Earl died in August, 1852 and, there being no heir, the estate and viscounty passed to a cousin who subsequently terminated all building projects.

Having heard of opportunities in the township of Melbourne, the newly unemployed Reed decided to try his luck and departed for Australia, arriving around July, 1853.

The city that Reed encountered was being rapidly transformed by one of the most lucrative gold rushes in history. Founded barely a decade and a half earlier, Melbourne's population had exploded from around 25,000 inhabitants in 1852, when gold was first discovered, to over 40,000 a year later.

This huge influx of people resulted in the construction of many new buildings in the township, the majority of which were single or two storey brick or timber structures, often of poor quality. The few public buildings that existed were modest in scale and stylistically outdated, such as the new town hall (1849-53) and the Supreme Court (1842-44). Melbourne's churches were similarly modestly sized and architecturally inspired by old-fashioned Regency Gothic and Classical trends.

For an ambitious and talented architect such as Reed, this increasingly wealthy young city must have seemed like an immense blank canvas upon which he could imprint a new, grander built environment.

ARCHITECTURE IN AUSTRALIA DURING THE MID TO LATE 19TH CENTURY GENERALLY FOLLOWED CONTEMPORARY TRENDS OF THE WESTERN WORLD, PARTICULARLY THOSE BEING PRACTICED IN THE U.K.

ARCHITECTURE IN THE 19TH CENTURY

Although the industrial revolution had advanced many architectural and structural technologies, enabling, for example, the increased use of steel and cast-iron, the majority of 19th century buildings still looked to the past for stylistic and decorative inspiration.

What is now termed Victorian architecture, referring to the reign of Queen Victoria (1837-1901), encompassed numerous historical interpretative and revival styles, ranging from Neo-Classical and Romanesque through to Gothic Revival and Beaux Arts.

Joseph Reed, utilising this eclectic range of styles, helped create an internationally renowned city that London journalist George Augustus Sala labelled in 1885 'Marvellous Melbourne'.

MARVELLOUS MELBOURNE

1 Cnr Flinders & Swanston Streets / 1891

ST PAUL'S CATHEDRAL

St Paul's Cathedral occupies the site of the first Christian service in Melbourne, conducted in 1835. The first substantial church building, a bluestone structure, was built on the site in 1852, followed in 1891 by the present building.

Neither Joseph Reed nor his firm had anything to do with the initial planning or design of the cathedral. The commissioned architect, Englishman William Butterfield, resigned from the project in 1888 (the foundation stone having being laid in 1880) and the firm now known as Reed, Henderson & Smart was invited to complete the building.

As the building was in such an advanced state of construction both the exterior and interior were, with a few exceptions, finished according to Butterfield's original designs.

OF NOTE

Flinders Street Station

Across from St Paul's, on the corner of Flinders and Swanston streets, is Flinders St Station, an iconic landmark familiar to all Melburnians. Completed in 1909 in a French Renaissance style, the main building features a prominent dome and arched entrance under which sit a row of clocks displaying departure times of the various train lines. "I'll meet you under the clocks" has hence become a popular Melbourne idiom.

Constructed of locally sourced sandstone, St Paul's is an example of Gothic Transitional architecture, being partly Early English and partly Decorated Gothic. The spires were a much later addition, designed by Sydney architect James Barr and constructed from 1926-1931.

The interior was inspired by the polychromatic treatment of Gothic Italian churches, evidenced in the horizontal banding running along the arches and walls of the nave. The pine ceiling, although finely executed, was not part of Butterfield's original plans.

The cathedral's pipe organ was built by T.C. Lewis and Co of Brixton, England and was played at the inaugural service in 1891.
It cost 6500 pounds including construction, shipping and installation.

WESTIN
LET'S
WELCOME
REFUGEES

2 15-17 Queen St / 1889

LOMBARD BUILDING

The Lombard Building was constructed in 1889 for Balfour, Elliott & Co. The seven storey structure is a good example of a late boom style design which incorporates a range of classical styles and decorative motifs intended to display the wealth of the owners.

The ornamentation increases as the building rises, culminating in a picturesque roofline with a pedimented parapet flanked by chimney stacks.

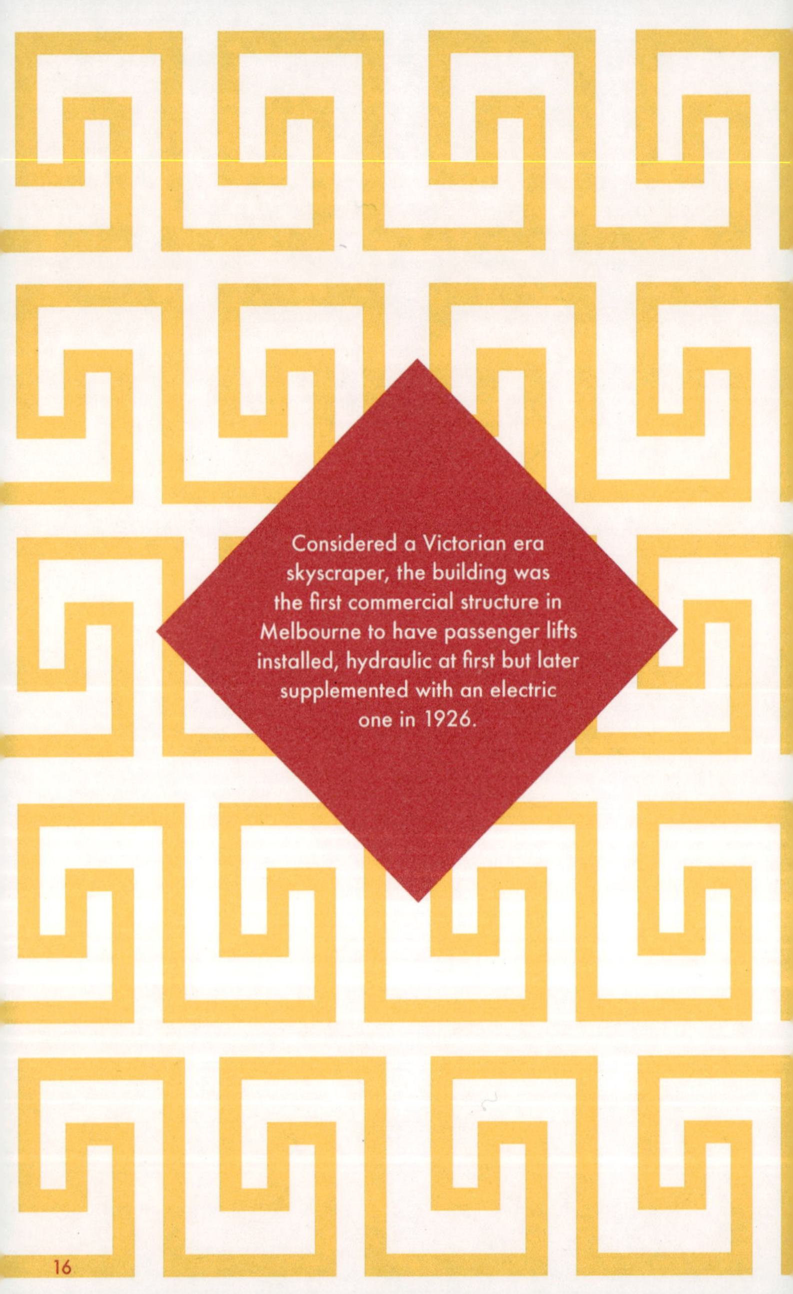
Considered a Victorian era skyscraper, the building was the first commercial structure in Melbourne to have passenger lifts installed, hydraulic at first but later supplemented with an electric one in 1926.

17

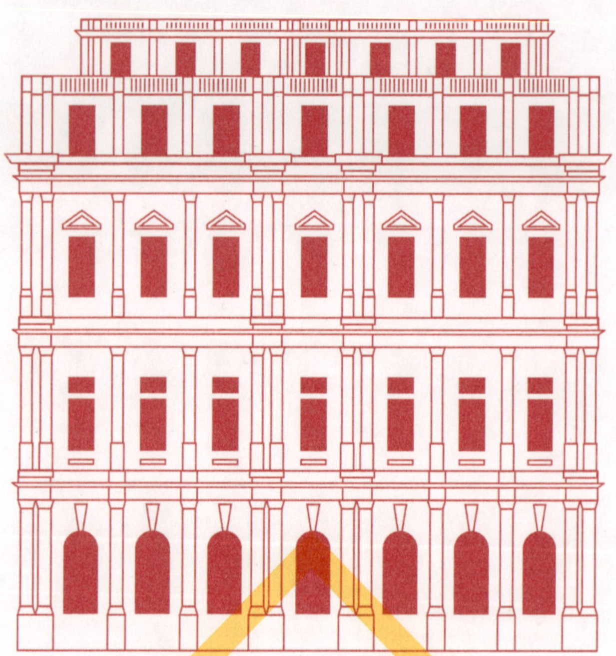

3 Cnr Collins & Queens Sts / 1876

BANK OF AUSTRALASIA

Founded in Sydney in 1835, the Bank of Australasia expanded rapidly, opening additional branches throughout Tasmania and then Melbourne in 1838. Due to the rapid growth of the city as a result of the gold rush, the bank decided to relocate its headquarters there, purchasing a prominent corner site in 1858.

Reed & Barnes had designed many branches for the Bank of Australasia throughout the 1870s and the headquarters building would be the largest of them. Completed in 1876, the original building had two storeys in the conservative Renaissance Revival style. The use of a Doric order for the pilasters and general lack of ornamentation lent a strong sobriety to the building, in keeping with the conservative nature of the banking firm itself. The grouping of pilasters at the corners, along with the prominent cornices, gave the impression of a classic three dimensional presence, even though only two facades are exposed.

In 1974 the bank, now known as the ANZ, sold the building after 98 years of occupancy. It now serves as an apartment hotel.

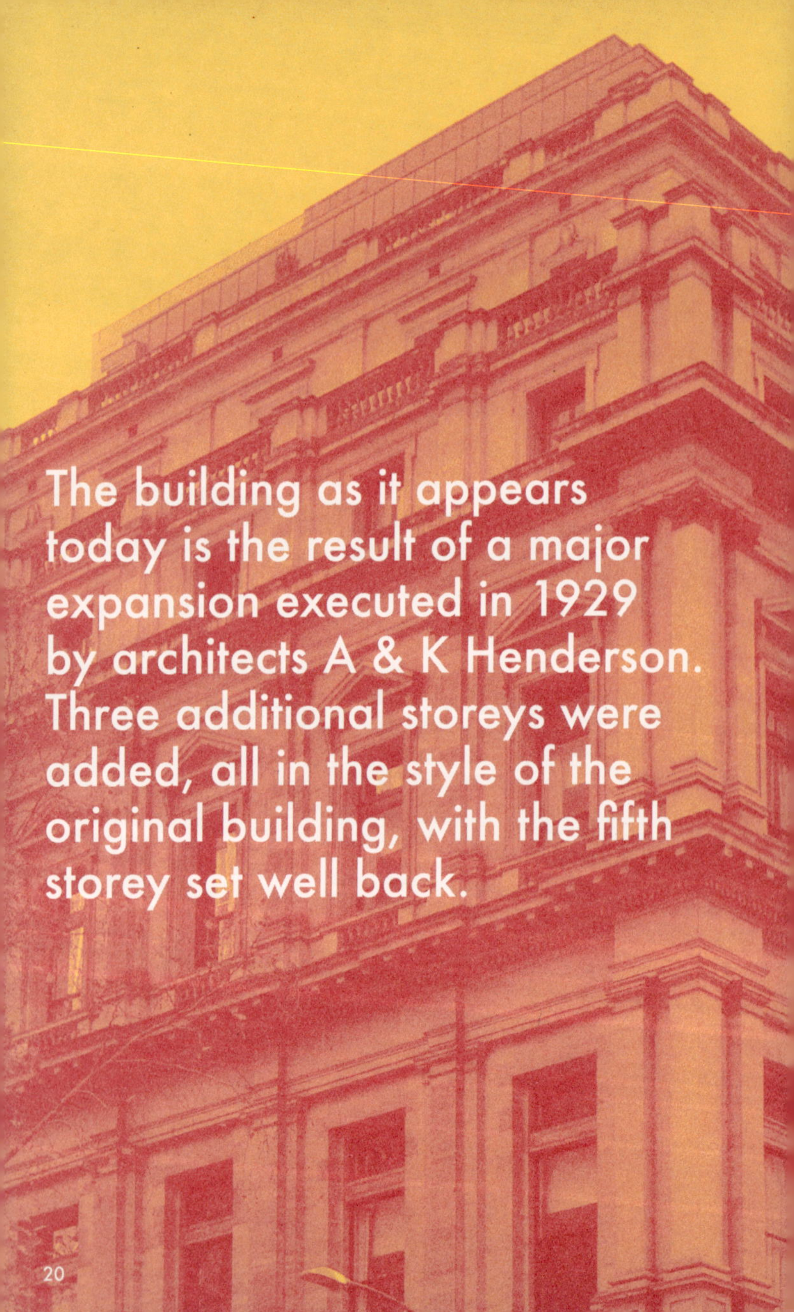

The building as it appears today is the result of a major expansion executed in 1929 by architects A & K Henderson. Three additional storeys were added, all in the style of the original building, with the fifth storey set well back.

✪ OF NOTE

ANZ Bank Building

Across from the Australasia building is the former English, Scottish and Australia Bank building, now occupied by ANZ Bank. Completed in 1887 to a design by architect William Wardell, it is considered the finest example of a secular Gothic Revival style in Australia.

OF NOTE

Block Arcade

Continuing on the suggested route to Melbourne Town Hall takes you to the Block Arcade, entered from either Collins or Elizabeth streets.

Designed by architect David C. Askew and completed in 1893, the arcade was intended to emulate the Galleria Emmanuele Vittoria in Milan, although on a much smaller scale.

Shops 1 and 2, near the Collins Street entrance, comprise the Hopetoun Tea Rooms, named after Lady Hopetoun. Established in 1891 for the Victorian Ladies Work Association, the tea rooms moved to their present location in 1907, having previously been located at shop number 6.

Serving the traditional 'high tea' for over 100 years (reservations required), the Hopetoun Tea Rooms is a lovely spot to sit down and relax with a beverage and fine food (regular menu available 7 days a week).

If something a little more substantial is required, exit onto Collins St, turn right and then right again into Block Court and you'll find the Charles Dickens Tavern. A basement pub with a quaint 19th century theme, it provides hearty meals and plenty of options to quench one's thirst.

Melbourne was officially incorporated as a town on 13th December 1842, but it would be over a decade before the first town hall was built. Completed in 1854, the modest brick building had been started four years previously but construction was delayed due to labour shortages as a result of the gold rush.

4 90-120 Swanston St / 1870

MELBOURNE TOWN HALL

The city was rapidly expanding in both size and wealth and, by the 1860s, it was decided that a new, grander structure, was more befitting of the most important public building in Melbourne. Reed & Barnes were chosen as the architectural firm to realise this ambition and their resulting design did not disappoint. The foundation stone was laid on 29th November 1867 by HRH Prince Alfred, Duke of Edinburgh (in Melbourne as part of his tour of Australia, the first such visit by British royalty), and the town hall officially opened on 9th August 1870 with a lavish ball.

Sitting on a rusticated bluestone base the Swanston and Collin Street facades feature a Classical Corinthian order of columns and pilasters. The central and corner pavilions are crowned with curved mansard roofs, a distinctive feature of French Second Empire architecture, a style very much in vogue at the time.

The clock tower (named Alfred Tower after HRH Prince Alfred) situated on the street corner continues the main structure's stylistic themes, with its stacked classical composition and smaller mansard roof.

The clocks themselves, built by Smith & Sons of London, were donated to the council by William Vallange Condell, the son of Melbourne's first mayor.

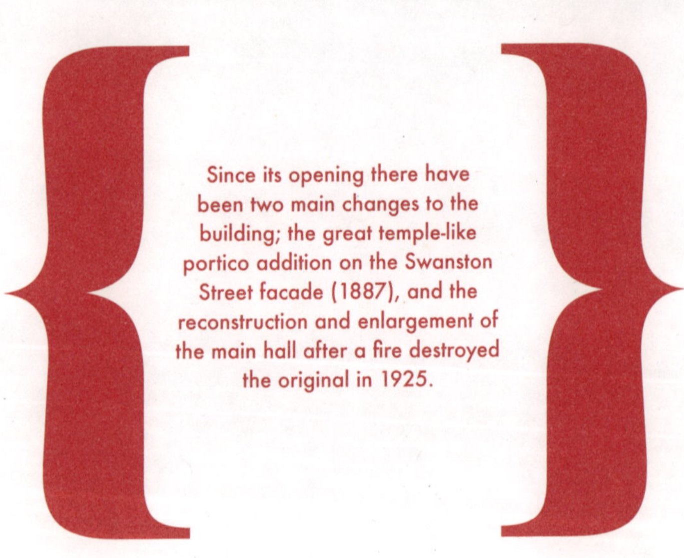
Since its opening there have
been two main changes to the
building; the great temple-like
portico addition on the Swanston
Street facade (1887), and the
reconstruction and enlargement of
the main hall after a fire destroyed
the original in 1925.

The original pipe organ
was also lost in the fire
and the present one,
comprising 6,024 pipes,
was manufactured by Hill,
Norman & Beard Ltd of
London in 1929.

In 1862 Reed formed a new architectural partnership with Frederick Barnes, who had been working in Reed's office since 1856. The new firm of Reed & Barnes swiftly got to work on a range of new projects, one of which was the Collins Street Baptist Church.

BAPTIST CHURCH

The first Baptist Church building in Victoria was founded on the Collins Street site in 1845, opposite the location of the first service, held in a tent in 1838. By the late 1850s a decision was made to enlarge the original building.

Unlike the usual Gothic or Romanesque treatment applied to many other churches of the period, Reed designed a Classical Roman style portico with large Corinthian columns. Reflecting the Baptist aversion to lavish decoration, the interior is finished in plain white plaster punctuated with arched windows. Seating is arranged around a double aisle facing the raised pulpit, with a gallery at the rear of the church supported by slender cast iron columns.

Opened in 1862, the church continues to play a significant role in Melbourne's Baptist community.

6 156 Collins St / 1874

SCOTS CHURCH

Executed in the English Decorated Gothic style, the Scots Church provides an interesting architectural contrast to the Romanesque Independent Church across the street. It also demonstrates Joseph Reed's great ability to work with the many and varied architectural styles of the time.

Completed in 1874, the building was the second Presbyterian Church to inhabit the corner site, the first being built in 1841. The decision to replace the original structure was made partly because of concerns with the structural integrity of the tower and spire which had developed large cracks, leading to a fear of collapse.

The new design was constructed using New Zealand limestone and locally sourced Barrabool sandstone from Geelong. The relatively austere interior is comprised of a spacious nave with large basalt columns lining the aisles. Dark timber panelling lines the walls which are punctuated by intricate, brightly coloured stained glass windows portraying various biblical themes.

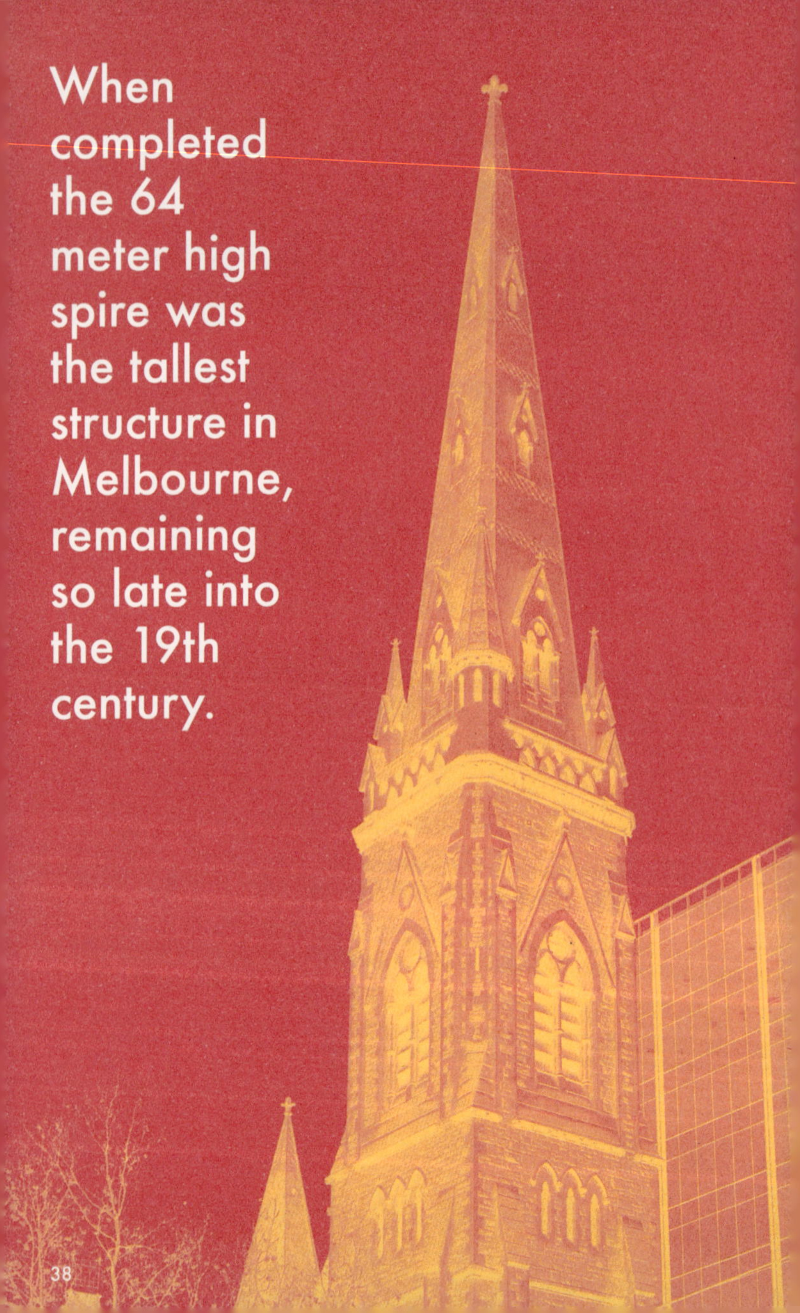
When completed the 64 meter high spire was the tallest structure in Melbourne, remaining so late into the 19th century.

The church's other notable claim to fame is that one of its choir members (the eldest daughter of the church's builder, David Mitchell) was later to become the famous operatic soprano, Dame Nellie Melba.

Late in 1862 Joseph Reed toured Europe, returning to Melbourne in October, 1863. His travels took him to the Lombardy region of Italy, known for its early Romanesque brick architecture. This visit inspired Reed to incorporate Italianate themes into many subsequent projects throughout the 1860s, one of which was the Independent Church (now St Michael's Uniting Church) on Collins St.

7 120 Collins St / 1867

INDEPENDENT CHURCH

The original Collins Street building was the first permanent church built in Melbourne (1839) and was demolished in 1866 to make way for Reed's design. The new church's Lombardic Romanesque design features polychrome brickwork, which was a first for Melbourne, having recently become popular in England with architects such as G.E Street and William Butterfield. The Italian inspired tower creates a dramatic visual presence, located as it is on the corner of two streets (Collins and Russell Streets), and flanked by the two main church facades.

This was the first realised campanile-like tower that Reed had built into one of his designs. He had previously incorporated towers in two architectural plans; one for an unsuccessful design submission for a new Government House (1864), the other for St Jude's Anglican Church in Carlton (1867) where the intended tower was omitted from the final built design.

The interior of the Independent Church was designed to maximise acoustic properties, comprising sloped, auditorium style seating above which sits a horseshoe shaped gallery. Ringed by large rounded Romanesque arches and slim iron columns, the entire space feels open and quite voluminous.

Taking less than a year to construct, the Independent Church was completed in August, 1867, the first service being conducted on the 25th of that month.

✪ OF NOTE

TREASURY BUILDING / PARLIAMENT HOUSE

Following the suggested route, you turn left from Collins St into Spring Street. The first building encountered across Spring Street is the Old Treasury Building, completed in 1862 and considered one of the finest Renaissance Revival structures in Australia. Designed by 19 year old architect J.J Clark, it was built from wealth gained through the Victorian gold rushes of the 1850s.

Further up Spring Street is Parliament House, completed over a protracted period from 1855 to 1929. Taking many design cues from Leeds Town Hall in the U.K, it is a fine example of Neoclassical architecture.

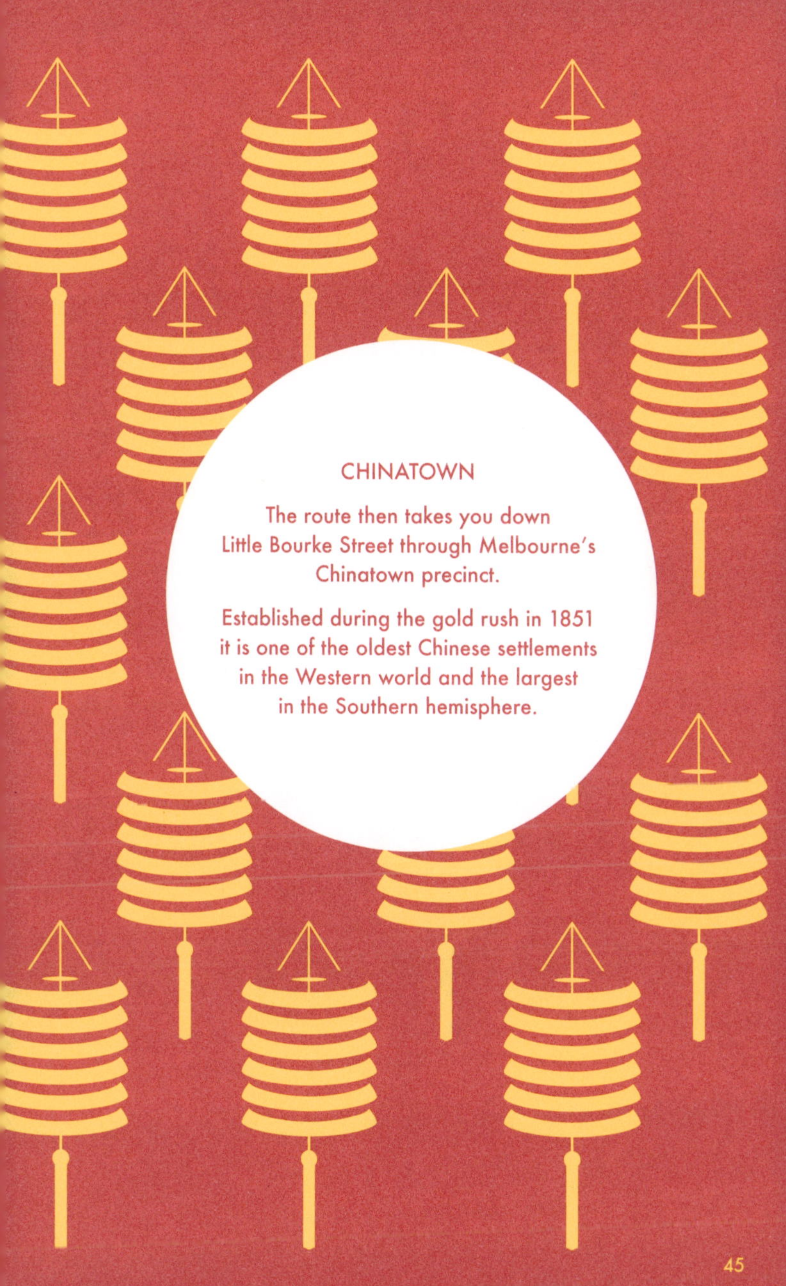

CHINATOWN

The route then takes you down Little Bourke Street through Melbourne's Chinatown precinct.

Established during the gold rush in 1851 it is one of the oldest Chinese settlements in the Western world and the largest in the Southern hemisphere.

8 148 Lonsdale St / 1857

WESLEY CHURCH

The Wesleyans (named after John Wesley, founder of the Methodist church) had been part of Melbourne's religious community since the beginning of European settlement, the first chapel being built on Collins Street in 1838.

In 1857 the chairman of the Methodist's Victorian district, Daniel Draper, proposed a new church building for Lonsdale Street and chose Joseph Reed as architect. Both Draper and Reed agreed on an English Gothic Revival style for the building, including a tall (53.3 metres) octagonal spire. This caused controversy amongst other Wesleyans with some criticising the design as being too Gothic, too ornate and even too Anglican. The plans remained unaltered, however, and the foundation stone was laid on December 2nd, 1857.

The exterior is constructed of bluestone with decorative freestone mouldings. The interior has a spacious nave surrounded by a gallery supported by slender columns. The pipe organ was the first of its kind in Melbourne, manufactured in England and arriving in the colony in 1842, being moved to Wesley Church in 1858.

9 9 Victoria St / 1859

ROYAL SOCIETY BUILDING

In 1855 the Philosophical Society of Victoria merged with the Victorian Institute for the Advancement of Science to form the Royal Society. The oldest learned society in Victoria, it has played an important role in the state's history including the establishment of the Melbourne Museum, organising the Burke and Wills expedition (1860-61) and, more recently, forming the Victorian Institute of Marine Sciences (1978).

In 1858 the society commissioned Joseph Reed to design a new headquarters, starting with a hall for meetings and lectures. Opened in December, 1859, the exterior was initially left in its unfinished, red brick state due to budget constraints. It was finally designed and rendered in the Academic Classical style in 1880, appearing as it does today. The original interior was a single rectangular hall, able to be divided by partitions for different purposes. From 1887 to 1889 this space was remodelled by Reed's firm, creating a separate second floor for the library and lecture theatre, with the Burke and Wills, Members' and Front rooms downstairs.

Further development was initiated in 1953 with an extension built onto the southern side of the building. This was carefully designed to match the existing style and created rooms for the Australian College of Obstetricians and Gynaecologists.

International Exhibitions, or 'World Fairs' as they would later be known, became immensely popular with industrialised nations throughout the 19th century.

Intended to promote international trade, showcase new technologies and instil national pride, the most famous of these events was arguably the 1851 'Great Exhibition of the Works of Industry of All Nations' held in the purpose built Crystal Palace in Hyde Park, London.

Throughout the 1870s the city of Melbourne made plans to organise and host its own international exhibition and, in December 1877, an architectural competition was announced for a purpose built venue. Eighteen firms entered and in May 1878 the submission from Reed & Barnes was declared the winner.

10 Carlton Gardens / 1880

ROYAL EXHIBITION BUILDING

The design of the Great Hall, the only surviving structure of the original exhibition complex, draws inspiration from an eclectic range of sources. The dome is modelled on that of Florence Cathedral by Brunelleschi, whilst the main pavilions display elements of the 19th century German Rundbogenstil style. Reed himself declared that the inspiration for many of the design elements came from the study of 15th century architecture in Normandy, Caen and Paris, in particular the projecting buttresses around the exterior of the building.

The hall and all adjoining buildings were completed in 1880, with the exhibition itself opening on October 1st. By the time it had finished on 30th April, 1881 over 1.4 million people had visited although the event made a loss of 277, 292 pounds.

The buildings were to host a number of significant events over the years including the Melbourne Centennial Exhibition (1888, celebrating 100 years since European settlement in Australia), the first Parliament of Australia (1901, following Federation) and as a venue for events of the 1956 Olympic Games (basketball, weightlifting and wrestling).

OF NOTE

Drummond Street

Drummond Street has one of the most concentrated collections of Victorian era residential housing in Melbourne. Many of the terrace style buildings have been renovated and display the beautiful intricate ironwork and exterior decoration that are the hallmarks of this architectural style.

Considered for demolition at various time during the 1950s and 60s, by the 1970s the heritage value of the building was finally being widely recognised and in 2004 it was listed as a World Heritage Site by UNESCO, a first for a building in Australia.

11 54 Victoria St / 1874

TRADES HALL

On 21st April 1856 stonemasons working on the Melbourne University site downed tools and marched to Parliament House, demanding the introduction of an eight hour workday. The government agreed to their demands and this significant victory led to the formation of organised trade unions throughout Victoria.

The first Trades Hall building was constructed on the Lygon Street site in 1859. A modest timber structure with a galvanised iron roof, it was fully funded by the workers themselves and remained on site until 1917, when it was removed to make way for further extensions to the present building.

Construction of the second, more substantial Trades Hall building began in 1874. Completed a year later, it was initially a relatively simple classical pavilioned two storey design featuring a Corinthian order. Between 1874 and 1925 there have been numerous additions to the original building, all designed by Reed & Barnes or its successors. The most dramatic feature, the large Roman style portico attached to the Lygon Street entrance, featuring eight large Corinthian columns, was added in 1917.

The oldest Trade Union building in the world, it still serves its original purpose, being home to numerous Victorian union and community organisations as well as serving as headquarters for the National Union of Students.

ABOR
888

Across from Trades Hall, on the corner of Lygon and Victoria streets, is a memorial to the Eight Hours Day movement. Originally unveiled on 21 April 1903 on Spring Street, it was relocated to its present location in 1924. The pedestal and column design is topped by three figure eights, representing (as inscribed on the globe sitting above) 8 hours rest, 8 hours work and 8 hours recreation.

✪ OF NOTE

Old Melbourne Gaol

Heading down Russell Street on the right hand side you pass the Old Melbourne Gaol, opened in 1845 and closed in 1929. Constructed in bluestone, the gaol was the scene of 133 executions, including the hanging of notorious Victorian bushranger Ned Kelly.

12 328 Swanston St / 1854

MELBOURNE PUBLIC LIBRARY

Shortly after arriving in Melbourne, Reed entered an architectural design competition for a new public library. He was announced as the winner in January 1854, and construction commenced in July with the laying of the foundation stone by Governor Sir Charles Hotham.

Facing Swanston Street, the library had a protracted construction period that stretched well into the 20th century. The central vestibule section was the first to be completed (1854-1858), followed by the south section (1859-63) and the north side (1864-65). The portico was added in 1869-70. The final design elements, the pavilion ends, were finished much later; the south wing in 1886 and the north wing in 1961.

The design itself was executed in a Roman Revival style using a Corinthian order, readily identified by the slender fluted columns topped by ornate capitals. It was possibly partly inspired by various contemporary U.K buildings, in particular Grosvenor House in London (home of the Grosvenor family, better known as the Dukes of Westminster).

Internally the ground floor consists of rooms on either side of the entrance hall, initially used for the display of various collections (coins, seals, medals etc.) and fine art illustrations. The most striking space, however, is the first floor library, named Queen's Hall. Running the full length of the double-height floor and lined with tall Ionic columns, this opulent, naturally lit space had a great impact on the public at the time.

Over the decades the site partly occupied by the library (bounded by Swanston, La Trobe, Russell and Little Lonsdale streets) has been developed and occupied by many institutions including the National Gallery of Victoria, the Industrial and Technological Museum and the Natural History Museum, all of which had buildings designed by Reed's practice and its successors. The most spectacular addition to the site, however, was the domed Reading Room, built as a new annexe to the library. Initiated by the library trustees in 1906, plans for the Reading Room were drawn up by the firm now known as Bates, Peebles and Smart, with the building being completed in 1913. Inspired by the U.S Congressional Library in Washington, the dome was briefly the largest reinforced concrete structure of its type in the world, measuring 34.75 metres in diameter.

Although altered at various times over the years, both the original library building and Reading Room remain beautiful and impressive examples of Melbourne's 19th and early 20th century built heritage.

The University of Melbourne was established by an act of the Victorian Parliament in 1853, making it the second oldest in Australia (the oldest being the University of Sydney, established 1850).

13 Melbourne Uni / 1881

ORMOND COLLEGE

When Melbourne University was established in 1853, ten acres of land each were allotted to various churches for the purpose of residential college accommodation.

Funded by the Presbyterian Church and wealthy pastoralist Francis Ormond, Ormond College opened in 1881 and, with over 400 students, is currently the largest of the university residential colleges.

Designed in the Gothic Revival style, the north-west wing was constructed in rough-hewn sandstone on a bluestone base, with cream brick dressings around windows and door openings. The tower, with its belfry and balcony, stands 50.3 metres high and is modelled after that of the University of Glasgow. Ormond College was one of many architectural commissions Reed undertook for the Presbyterian Church throughout the 1870s and 1880s. They included three churches at Koroit (1870), Horsham (1873) and Prahran (1875) and Presbyterian Ladies College in East Melbourne (1874, demolished).

Ormond College was the largest, however, and is widely considered the finest example of these projects.

Over the years various major and minor additions have been made to the college including the south-west wing (1885-87), Allen House (1892-93), the south-east wing (1922) and, more recently, McCaughey Court (1969).

BANK OF NSW FACADE

In 1856 the bank of New South Wales held a design competition for a new head office in Collins Street. Joseph Reed was chosen as the winning architect, his second competition success in as many years.

The two storey facade was done in the Renaissance Revival style with Ionic order columns placed at street level whilst, on the upper level, Corinthian columns are capped with an ornate entablature. Each level includes an intricate frieze carved by sculptor Charles Summers, the upper frieze depicting cherubs carrying floral garlands, the lower decorated with ornamented wreaths.

Although Reed's designs were rarely directly inspired by existing buildings, the bank of NSW takes many cues from the Italian Renaissance Library of St Mark in Venice (1553, Jacopo Sansovino).

Unfortunately by 1861 internal structural problems had been discovered and, by 1885, the building was in need of extensive repairs and restoration. Further deterioration of the facade, coupled with the bank's need for expansion, resulted in the building's demolition in 1932, to be replaced by an Art Deco design in 1936.

The building's facade, however, was saved and subsequently gifted by the bank to the University of Melbourne where it stands today. It forms the west facing facade of the school for Architecture, Building and Planning.

GATEKEEPER'S COTTAGE

In 1858 the university appointed Joseph Reed as its official architect, his first project being for a new gatekeeper's cottage located at the main entrance on Grattan Street. The former building had burned down in 1856 and by 1860 Reed had completed designs for a two room cottage in the Picturesque Gothic style. Sitting on a bluestone base, the walls are composed of straw-coloured bricks with sandstone decorative elements, upon which sit steeply pitched roofs clad in slate.

Throughout the 20th century alterations were made to the building, including filling in the veranda, an iron security door and, in 1962, an extension to the west side for a laundry, bathroom and porch.

In addition to being the second earliest surviving building on campus (the Old Quadrangle being the oldest) the cottage is also the earliest brick structure.

✪ OF NOTE

Wilson Hall

Impressed by Sydney University's 'Great Hall', Melbourne University Chancellor Redmond Barry decided that his institution must have a similarly grand structure. Funded by a generous 30,000 pound bequest from wealthy pastoralist Samuel Wilson, the grand hall was constructed from 1879-1882 to a design by Reed & Barnes. With its large pointed arches, elaborate timber roof trusses and emphasis on vertical and horizontal lined window tracery, the original hall was a dramatic example of the Perpendicular Gothic style.

Used primarily for the university's ceremonial activities, the hall was destroyed by a fire in 1952. The present Wilson Hall (1956) stands above its predecessor's foundations and was designed by the firm which evolved from Reed & Barnes, that of Bates, Smart & McCutcheon.

MELBOURNE CEMETERY

Across from the Melbourne University colleges on College Crescent is Melbourne Cemetery, a 43 hectare necropolis that was established in 1852.

Featuring many heritage structures including chapels and cast iron pavilions, the cemetery is also the final resting place for many prominent Victorians including Robert O'Hara and William John Wills (of the doomed Burke & Wills expedition) and Peter Lalor of Eureka Stockade fame.

WHELAN THE WRECKER

Established in the early 1890s by James Paul Whelan, the Whelan the Wrecker demolition company was responsible for the destruction of thousands of structures across Melbourne throughout the 20th century. Seen as harbingers of urban progress by some and architectural vandals by others, the company gained notoriety throughout the 1950s, 60s and 70s as the most visible demolisher of Victorian era buildings in the city with its 'Whelan the Wrecker is Here' signs posted at its sites.

Although there was general public apathy towards this architecture in the early post-war years, the situation wasn't helped by a City of Melbourne by-law (1954) that called for the removal of all Victorian era cast-iron verandas from street frontages. This was ostensibly for the safety of pedestrians but was also seen as a way to 'modernise' the Melbourne streetscape, especially with the 1956 Olympic Games looming. Unfortunately this often resulted in the removal of entire buildings along with the offending verandas.

However it also sparked an architectural preservation movement which in turn led to the establishment of non-government bodies such as the National Trust of Victoria (founded in 1956), an organisation that has helped save numerous historically significant buildings in Melbourne.

JOSEPH REED TIMELINE

1837 Sir Richard Bourke, Governor of New South Wales, approves the site for what will become the settlement of Melbourne. Robert Hoddle is shortly thereafter assigned the task of surveying the area and lays out the grid for the proposed city.

1851 Gold is discovered in the Victorian town of Clunes, sparking one of the biggest gold rushes in history.

1858 The first recorded game of Australian Rules Football is played between Scotch College and Melbourne Grammar.

1865 Melbourne overtakes Sydney as Australia's most populous city.

1878 The telephone is used for the first time in Melbourne.

1880 Melbourne hosts the World's Fair in the purpose-built Exhibition Buildings in Carlton Gardens.

1885 Impressed by the grand architecture, visiting English journalist George Augustus Henry Sala coins the phrase "Marvellous Melbourne".

1891 A period of great prosperity leads to wild land and property speculation. The inevitable financial bust that follows plunges Melbourne and Victoria into a severe depression.

1901 Federation of Australian colonies. Melbourne is nominated the new nation's seat of government, remaining so until 1927 when Canberra becomes the country's capital.

Buttress: A structure of masonry or brick used to provide lateral support to a wall

Campanile: Italian term for bell tower

Classical Order: A principal component of classical architecture comprising base, shaft, capital and entablature

Corinthian: One of the five classical orders, characterized by acanthus leaves decorating the capitals

Entablature: The structure above the capital comprising architrave, frieze and cornice

Facade: An exterior side of a building, often referring to the front

Freestone: A soft stone used in masonry for carving, moulding and tracery (eg sandstone)

Frieze: The central component of the entablature, often decorated with a relief design

Gallery: A platform raised above a church floor

Ionic: One of the five classical orders, characterised by a scroll like ornament decorating the capital and often fluted shaft

Mansard: French style four-sided roof

Nave: The main body of a church building

Parapet: A vertical extension of the facade wall at the edge of a roof

Pavilion: A structural emphasis placed at the end of a symmetrical building's wings

Pediment: A classical triangular shaped structure placed above the entablature of a building

Pilasters: A column feature projecting from the face of a wall (as opposed to a free standing column)

Portico: A porch extending from the main body of a building

Pulpit:The raised stand for speakers in a church

Rundbogenstil: 19th century Romanesque revival style popular in German speaking nations

Vestibule: A small room or hall between the entrance and the interior of a building

THE WALK

The Footpath Guide to Joseph Reed architecture in Melbourne takes approximately 1.5 to 2 hours to complete.